This book belongs to:
(Write your name in the palms of my hands)

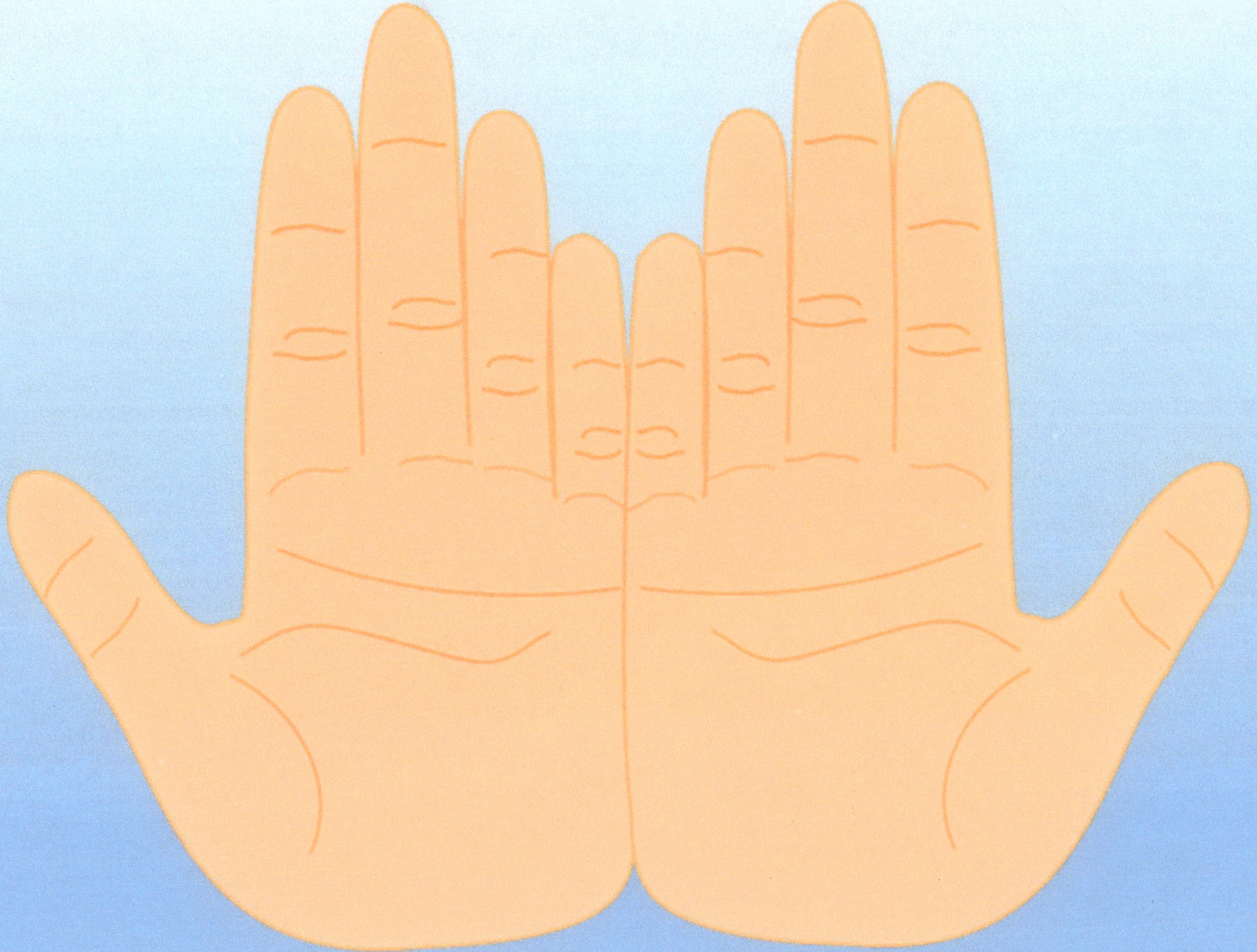

 I thank God my name is written on the palms of His hands . . . -- Isaiah 49:16 (NLT)

The Lost Pumpkin's Halloween Adventure

(Adapted From The Lost Son Parable From The Gospel of Luke)

W&D Parables

Written and Illustrated by
Wanda Hernandez

Copyright © 2018 by Wanda Hernandez.
Illustrated by Wanda Hernandez.

All rights reserved. This book or any portion thereof may not be reproduced or used in any form or manner whatsoever without the express written permission of the publisher except for the use of brief quotations in a book review.

October 2018

Library of Congress Control Number: 2018909406

ISBN 978-0-692-16936-0 (paperback)

Wanda Hernandez
Bronx, New York

10 9 8 7 6 5 4 3 2 1

Acknowledgments

I thank the greatest creator who inspired me and taught me how to stretch my gift of creativity, my Father God. I also thank Him that He blessed me with this good and perfect gift from above. It is a pleasure to write and draw for His glory. I am truly blessed!

I thank my daughter, Danielle, who got the ball rolling with her sixth grade pumpkin essay.

This story is based on The Prodigal Son parable in Luke 15:11-32 of The Holy Bible and does not in any way support Halloween! It's to remind everyone that God loves you no matter what.

Scriptures are from The New Century Version bible (NCV),
The Living Bible (TLB) and the Good News Translation (GNT).

Hello, I'm Light. When you see me, you will see God's promises. Read His promises out loud everyday.

 It won't be me talking—it will be the Spirit of my heavenly Father speaking through me! — Matthew 10:20

GOD'S PROMISE OF HIS LOVE FOR YOU

Dear Child,

I promise you that neither death, nor life, nor angels, nor ruling spirits, nothing now, nothing in the future, no powers, nothing above you, nothing below you, nor anything else in the whole world will ever be able to separate you from my love that is in Christ Jesus our Lord.

Much Love,
Your Heavenly Father

-- Romans 8:38,39

It's a sunset night
and it's Halloween,
on a quiet farm sat
a young pumpkin.

So he made up his mind
   to leave this farm life behind
and he came up to his dad to say,
   "Dad, I've been thunkin,"
said the young pumpkin
   "That it's time I leave home today.

Halloween is where a pumpkin should be
with cool friends who know how to have fun.
No need to worry about me
because I got money
and I'm real smart too," said his son.

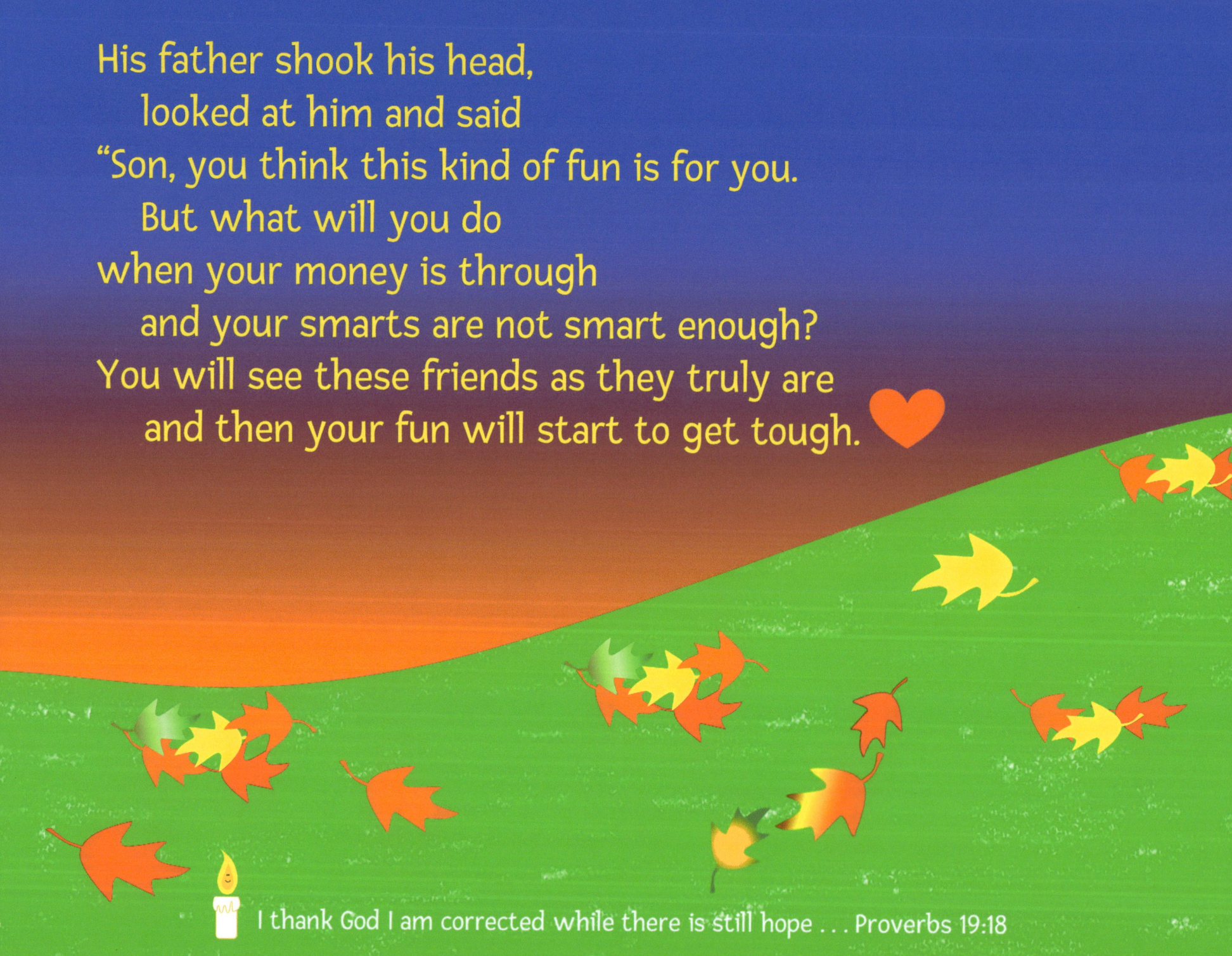

His father shook his head,
    looked at him and said
"Son, you think this kind of fun is for you.
    But what will you do
when your money is through
    and your smarts are not smart enough?
You will see these friends as they truly are
    and then your fun will start to get tough.

I thank God I am corrected while there is still hope . . . Proverbs 19:18

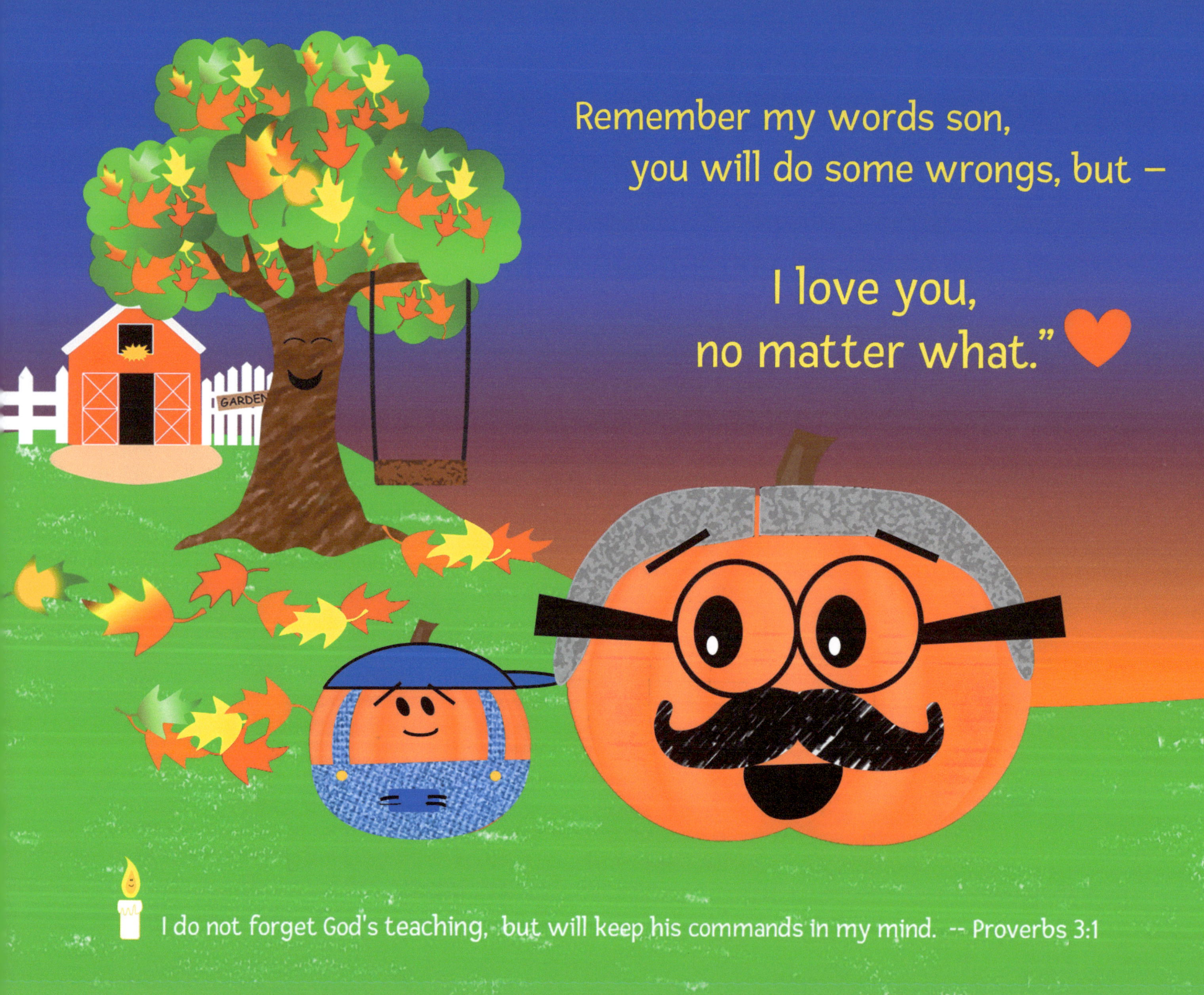

Soon he came to the place called Foolishness
and could not believe the sights.
So many strangers and fast flying things
and all kinds of spooky lights.

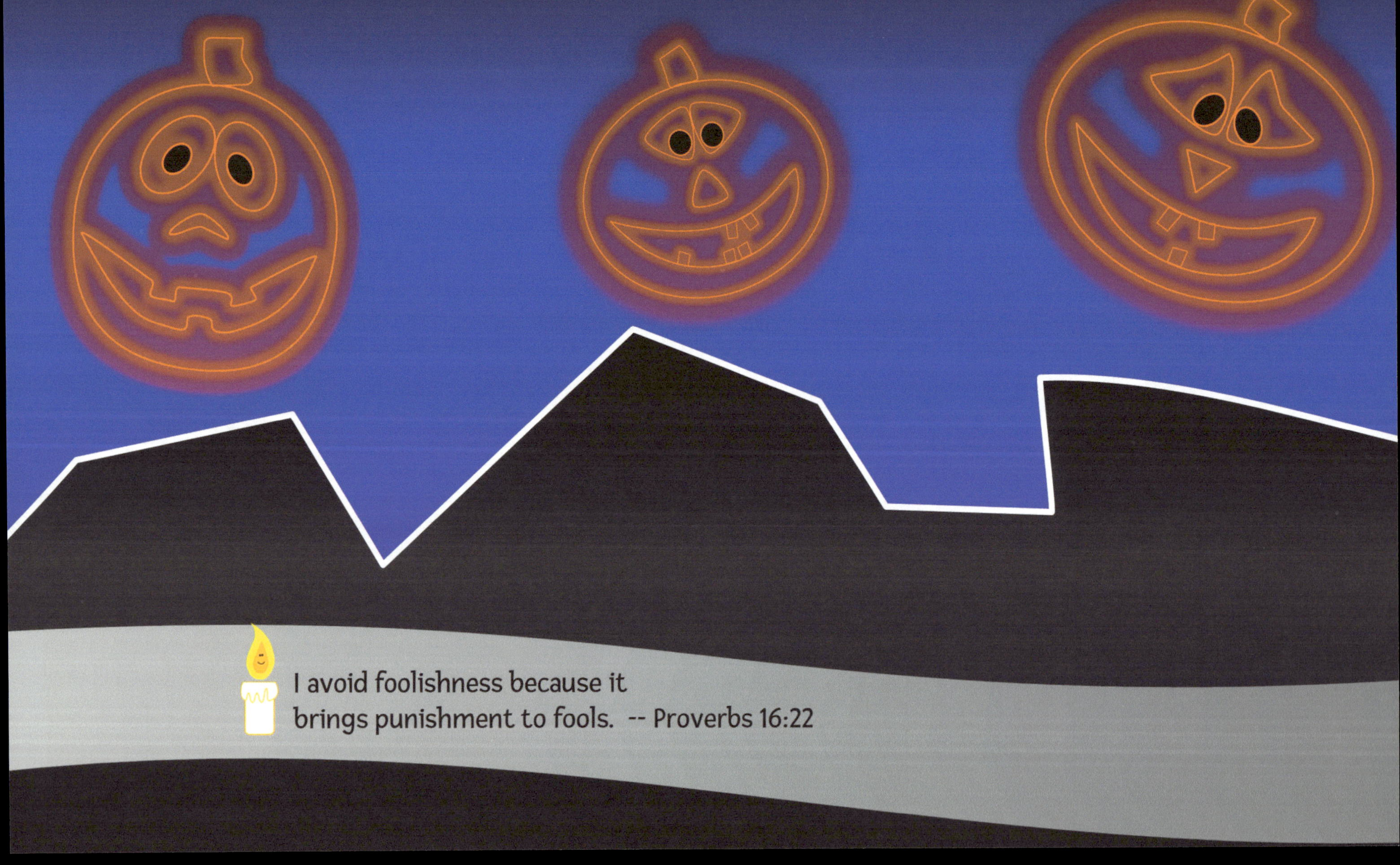

I avoid foolishness because it
brings punishment to fools. -- Proverbs 16:22

While the young pumpkin
   was staring and thunkin',
a large dooming figure appeared.
   He seemed to be nice,
was smooth and fast talking
   and he smiled a very slick leer.

"Here in Foolishness,
it's the right place to be.
You'll have lots of fun and great laughter.
You have to be smart and have plenty of money. Trust me, I know the thrills you're after."

Soon he made new friends
and he tricked and he treated
and spent all of his playing money.
He played all night and had lots of fun
with his new friend named Sonny.

Next morning, Jack O' Lantern shook him real hard and yelled to him to wake up! He snarled "you made your friends and had your fun and now my pay I must take up!"

But his friends laughed and yelled at him
"Come back when you get more money."
They pushed him away and left him alone
including his new friend named Sonny.

 Some people pretend to be my friends, but a real friend will be more loyal than a brother. – Proverbs 18:24

The young pumpkin had enough of this fun,
he knew this life was wrong.
He rolled quickly away without saying a word,
back home where he knew he belong.

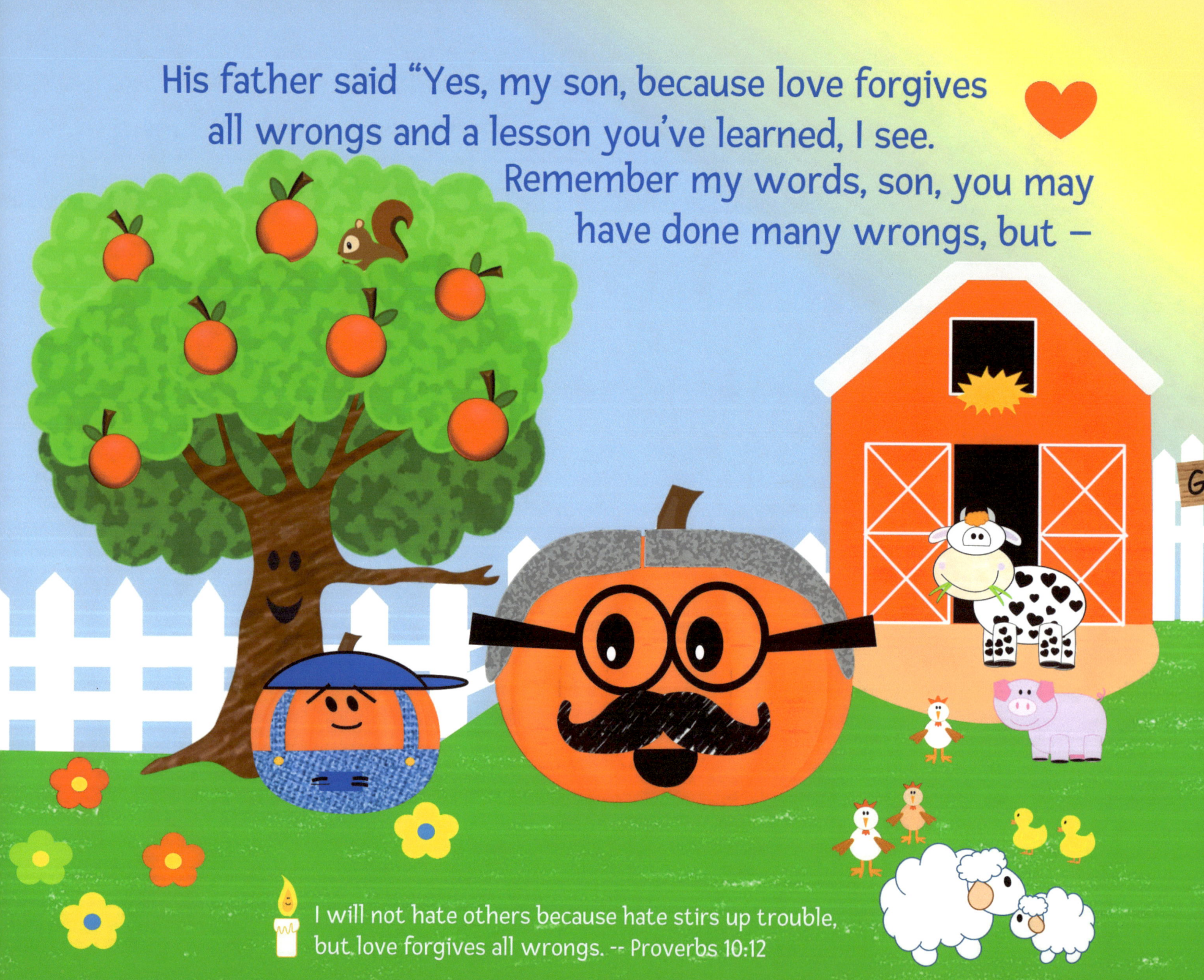

"I love you, no matter what."

I am a good child and that makes my father very happy; my parents are glad because I am wise. -- Proverbs 23:24

THE END

COME TO JESUS

(confess aloud)

Dear Heavenly Father,

I come to you in the name of your son, Jesus, and ask you to forgive me of my sins so that I can be right with you. I believe that Jesus died for my sins and that you raised Him from the dead.

Come into my heart Jesus, to be my Lord and savior. I know I am saved. I am now a child of God in your holy name. Amen.

If I confess that Jesus is Lord and believe that God raised Him from death, I will be saved. For it is by my faith that I am put right with God; it is by my confession that I am saved. – Romans 10:9,10

LET'S TALK ABOUT IT

<u>What Do You Think?</u> Was the father right to forgive his son even though his son did not listen to him? Why? Do you forgive all wrongs?

Did you see these  in the story? That part of the story shows an example of God's love for you.

Can you find other places in this story of God's love? What other examples of God's love can you find in the Holy Bible?

▶ YouTube   If you enjoyed this story, watch other W&D Parables stories on YouTube. Please give it a like and a comment! I would like to hear from you!

New Book Coming Soon!

What Can I Do?

I speak wise words and teach others to be kind. -- Proverbs 31:26

www.ingramcontent.com/pod-product-compliance
Lightning Source LLC
Chambersburg PA
CBHW041326290426

44110CB00004B/148